COLOR THEORY 101

POCKET GUIDE

TABLE OF CONTENTS

01 WHAT IS COLOR THEORY?

Color theory is the study of color: how to mix colors to form new colors, how to evoke specific emotions or symbols with color, the relationships between various colors, and how colors might compare or contrast against one another. Color theory has been used for centuries by working artists all over the world.

Although applying color theory traditionally has been seen as an artform, it has become more formalized over the years and is now often thought of as a science, too. We'll discuss the differences between the tradition and science of studying color later in this guide.

WHY DOES COLOR THEORY MATTER?

Color theory matters because the significance of color goes beyond just enhancing a piece of art. Color communicates feelings and messages to the viewer, it's like a visual language of its own. Think of how the red, yellow, and green colors within a traffic light are crucial to telling drivers when to speed up, slow down, or stop at a busy intersection.

HOW THE HUMAN EYE PERCEIVES COLOR

The human eye contains millions of light-sensitive cells called cones and rods. Cones enable you to detect red, green, and blue light. Rods work to primarily detect light and assist with night vision. When light enters the eye, it is then sent to the brain, which interprets the information and creates the sensation of color. The way you perceive color can be influenced by external factors, such as lighting and nearby surrounding colors, as well as internal factors like your thoughts or emotional state.

THE COLOR SPECTRUM AND THE VISIBLE LIGHT SPECTRUM

The **color spectrum** is the range of colors that can be seen when picked up by the cones in the human eye. It includes all the colors from violet to red, which you can see in a rainbow or when light is refracted through a prism. This **visible spectrum** of light wavelengths is only a small part of the electromagnetic spectrum, which also includes invisible light, like ultraviolet and infrared rays.

HUE, SATURATION, AND VALUE

Hue refers to the color itself, usually the purest version of a color. You could also say something like "purplish crimson hue" to describe a more complicated color.

Saturation refers to the intensity or purity of a color. A color with high saturation is brighter and more vivid, while a color with low saturation is more muted. Some color models refer to saturation as "chroma." You can mix gray into a pure color to make it less saturated and add more of the pure color to increase the saturation.

Notice how the red color becomes gradually less and less saturated as more gray is introduced along the gradient. At the right end of the gradient the red is completely desaturated and turns into solid gray.

Value refers to how light or dark the color is. If a color is mixed with white, it will become lighter or higher in value. If mixed with black, it becomes darker or lower in value.

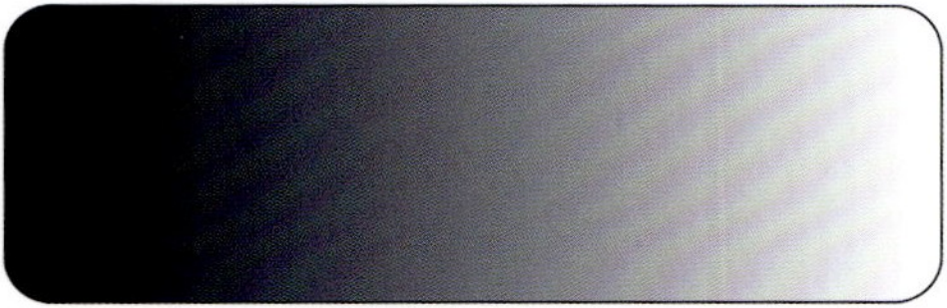

Notice how the black becomes gradually lighter and eventually turns to white as the gradient goes from left to right.

SHADES, TINTS, AND TONES

A **shade** is any amount of black plus a base color. Due to the addition of black, a shade will be darker than the base color.

A **tint** is any amount of white plus a base color. Due to the addition of white, a tint will be lighter than the base color.

Tone is any amount of gray plus a base color. The more gray you add to a color, the less saturated it becomes, so tones tend to be more muted colors.

MONOCHROMATIC VS. CONTRASTING COLORS

A **monochromatic** color palette is one that features various tints, shades, and tones of the same base color.

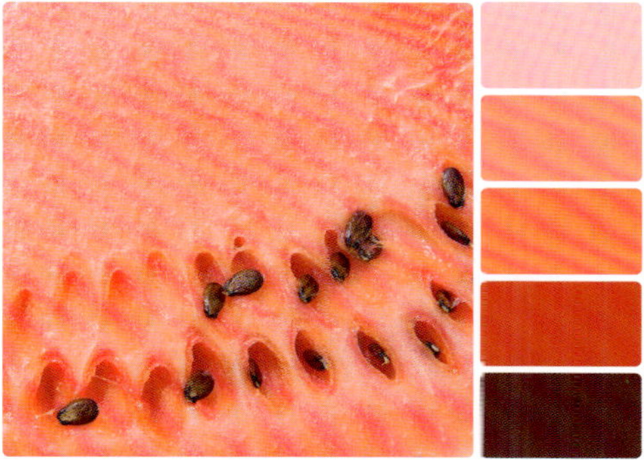

This image showcases a monochromatic palette of multiple shades of watermelon pink ranging from light pink to red to burgundy.

This ensures that the composition is harmonious and has no clashing colors. But some might argue that a monochromatic work of art lacks visual interest.

Using Contrasting Colors

Contrast is a stark difference between two or more colors when placed next to one another. The more dissimilar the colors are to one another, the higher the contrast. Low contrast is when all the colors in a composition are similar to one another. Low-contrast colors have a unifying effect, while high-contrast colors create tension and movement.

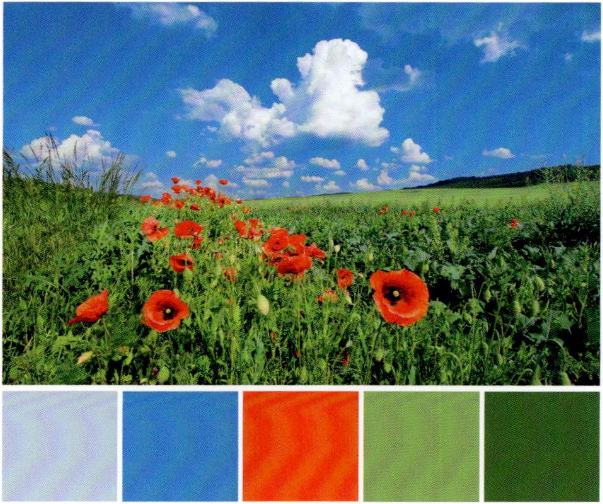

In this image, the bright orange-red poppy stands out against the green grass.

Using a palette of contrasting colors can have the opposite effect of a monochromatic palette.

Visibility

Artwork with high-contrast colors tend to be more visible from long distances, while low-contrast colors tend to blend together and be less visible from far away.

High visibility is important in situations where legibility is a priority. For example, graphic designers typically incorporate high-contrast colors whenever working with lettering. Signage is always clearer for a reader when contrast is as high as possible. This is why most text is written in black against a white or light-colored background.

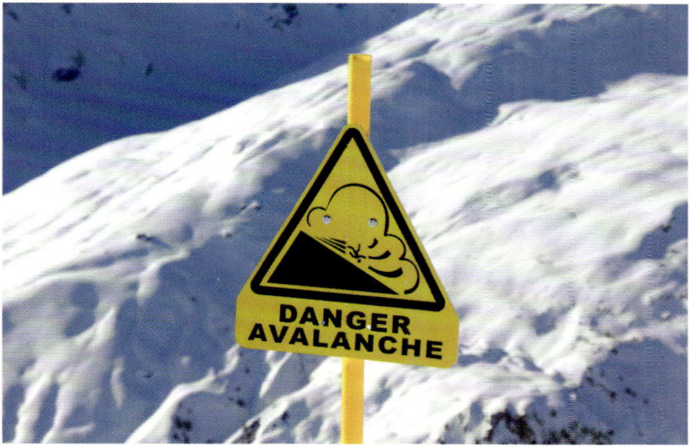

This bright yellow sign is highly visible against the surrounding snow and features clear, black lettering, making it easy to read.

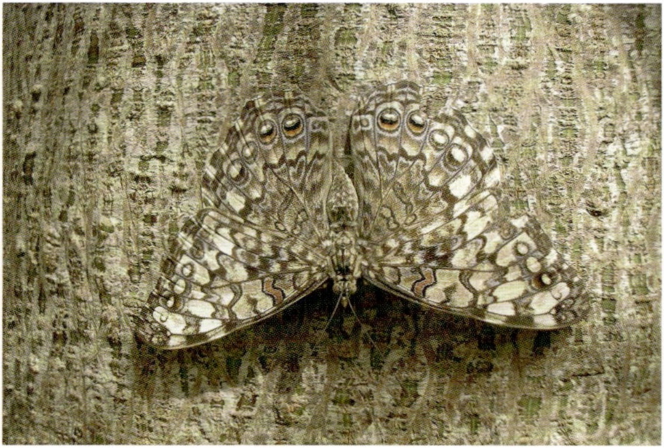

The concept of camouflage relies on using low-contrast colors that are similar to one another to conceal someone or something by blending into an environment.

Using vibrant colors that oppose each other on the color wheel can make for art that is vibrant and dynamic, but some might argue that this can also make a piece feel too busy or chaotic.

Monochromatic colors tend to blend together and be less visible from long distances, while contrasting colors usually have higher visibility. This is why lots of street signs feature designs with bright or contrasting colors.

02 THE COLOR WHEEL

The **color wheel** (sometimes called the "color circle") is made up of 12 colors organized into three categories: primary colors, secondary colors, and tertiary colors. You can use it as a guide to see how these colors relate to one another. Artists use the color wheel to help them make informed choices about the colors in their artwork.

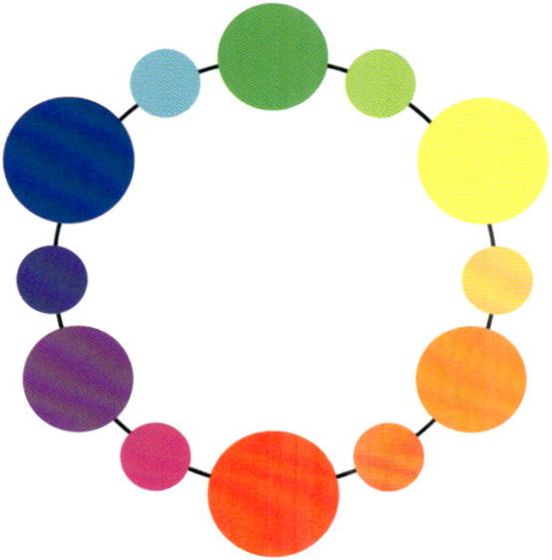

While the study and theory of color has existed since antiquity, a rough version of the color wheel as we know it was first seen in 1704. It was featured in a publication written by Issac Newton called *Opticks: or, A Treatise of the Reflexions, Refractions, Inflexions and Colours of Light.*

THE PRIMARY COLORS

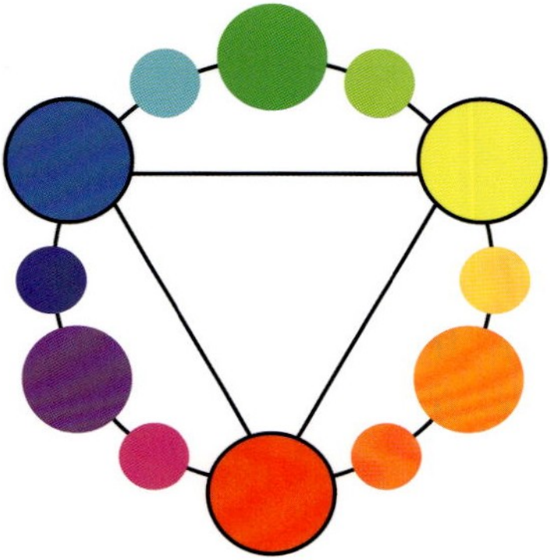

The three primary colors are red, yellow, and blue. These three basic colors are the building blocks to create all other colors. The points of each primary color form a triangle on the color wheel.

THE SECONDARY COLORS

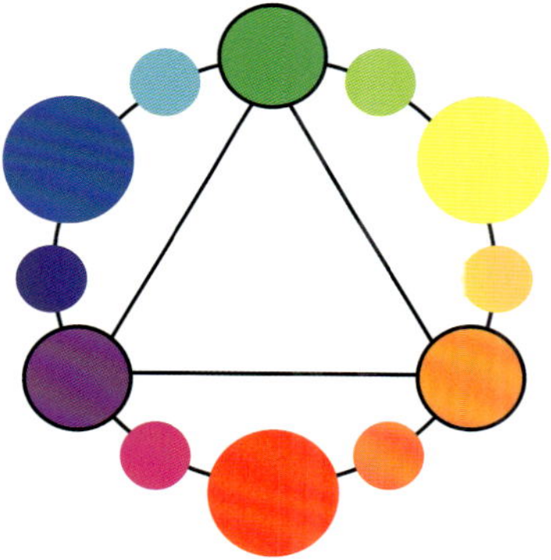

The secondary colors are green, purple, and orange. These three colors are made by combining two primary colors together. Green is made by mixing yellow and blue. Purple is made by mixing red and blue. Orange is made by mixing red and yellow. Just like the primary colors, the points of each secondary color form a triangle on the color wheel.

TERTIARY COLORS

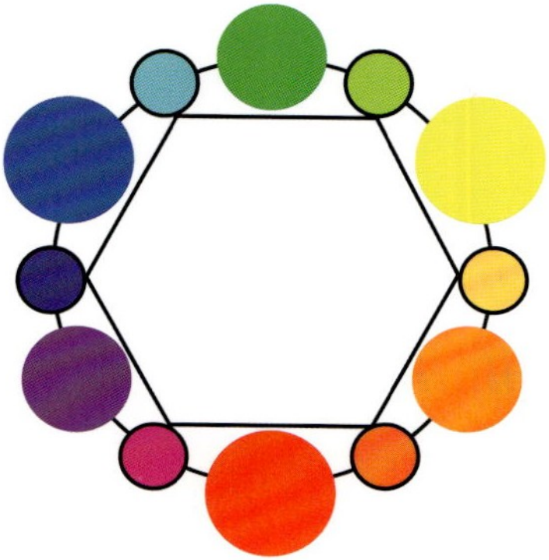

Tertiary colors are made by combining one primary color and one secondary color. These colors are showcased in the smallest circles of the example color wheel. The tertiary colors are teal (blue green), chartreuse (yellow green), amber (yellow orange), vermillion (orange red), magenta (red purple), and violet (blue purple).

03 COLOR PSYCHOLOGY AND SYMBOLISM

There's a difference between studying the symbolism of color theory versus studying the psychology of color theory. Let's break these differences down so you can understand how to implement them in your own work.

COLOR PSYCHOLOGY

A scientific approach to the study of color, **color psychology** aims to understand the ways in which color can influence human thought and behavior. Experimentation finds evidence of the effect of colors on people in specific conditions. It's objective and data driven.

For example, scientific research is helping us better understand how color impacts the brain in prison communities and the food industry.

Research by Dr. Alexander Schauss, head of the American Institute for Biosocial Research, shows that when prison inmates wear pink jumpsuits or are placed in cells where the walls are painted pink, the color lowers blood pressure and can have a sedating effect that reduces prisoner violence overall.

Research participants consistently rate foods with warm colors as more appetizing than cool-toned foods. Marketing firms are very aware of this fact, which is why most fast-food chains use yellow, orange, or red in their branding. Conversely, the color blue is very rarely seen in the foods that humans eat. Because of this, it has been known to have an appetite suppressing effect, so it is very rarely used in restaurant and food branding.

COLOR SYMBOLISM

Symbolism is a more historical and representative approach to the study of color. While some color meanings are more or less universally accepted, others can vary depending on a country, ethnicity, or religion. In other words, the same color can have radically different meanings depending on the context—so make sure you research and choose your colors carefully with this in mind.

In many cultures, for example, white symbolizes purity, but in some Asian countries it is the color of mourning, worn at funerals by grieving family members. People from these cultures may associate white with death.

Here are some common, widely accepted color symbols:

- **Yellow:** Happiness, positivity, exuberance
- **Orange:** Creativity, innovation
- **Red:** Danger, lust, survival
- **Green:** Nature, healing, growth
- **Blue:** Sadness, self-reflection
- **Violet:** Spirituality, royalty, mystery

Symbolism is more subjective than psychology and is, therefore, more open to personal interpretation. Feel free to use and create your own symbolic associations for colors within your art.

MOOD

Now that you've learned about color symbolism and color psychology, it's time to think about the emotions or ideas you want someone to feel or think when they view your work. Do you want your viewer to feel sadness? Disgust? Hope? Joy? Is the subject of your work a tranquil river in a wintertime landscape or a stoic portrait of an elderly couple? How would you approach your color choices in each scenario? Would they be different?

There are no right or wrong answers to these questions. Odds are that multiple approaches could work. The key is being thoughtful in how your color application can support the message you are trying to relay to the world.

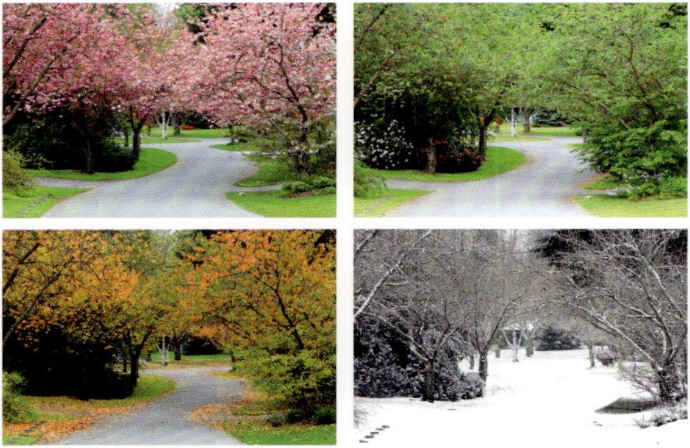

These four images depict the same place at different times of the year. Consider how the color palette of each season influences the mood of the environment.

04 CHOOSING COLORS FOR HARMONY OR CONTRAST

Color harmony is when all the colors in an art piece work together to create a balanced, visually appealing design. Color harmony is usually the goal for most artists. Some ways to achieve color harmony include choosing analogous color schemes and making sure your colors aren't too saturated or intense.

Color clashing is the opposite of color harmony and occurs when two or more colors in an art piece create a sort of visual conflict. Sometimes these clashes can even cause eye strain to a viewer. This is usually achieved by combining colors that are high contrast or opposite to one another on a color wheel or using lots of bright or neon colors.

Color clashes in art are not inherently "bad." They can make for very bold and interesting work and have been utilized more and more in contemporary and modern art. That said, if you decide to use colors that clash in your work, choose the colors carefully and make sure that your choices make sense within the context of the art.

TEMPERATURE

Color temperature refers to how cool or warm the undertones of a color are. A warm temperature means that a color is made up of mostly pure red or pure yellow. A cool temperature means that a color is primarily made up of mostly pure blue.

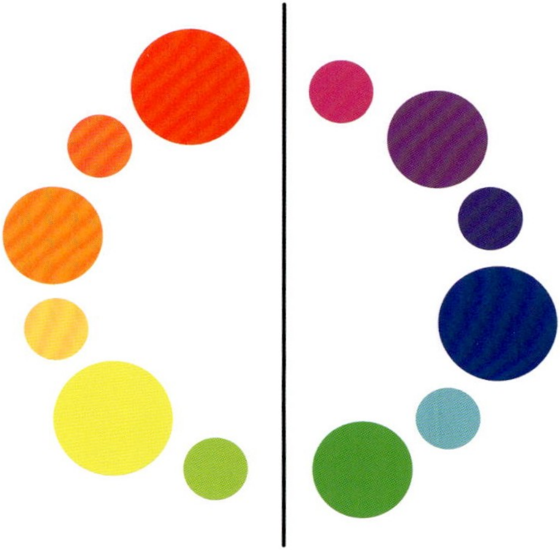

This color wheel is divided into two sides: warm colors on the left and cool colors on the right.

Because magenta and green contain both warm and cool colors, they can be considered either warm or cool depending on how much blue, yellow, or red they have.

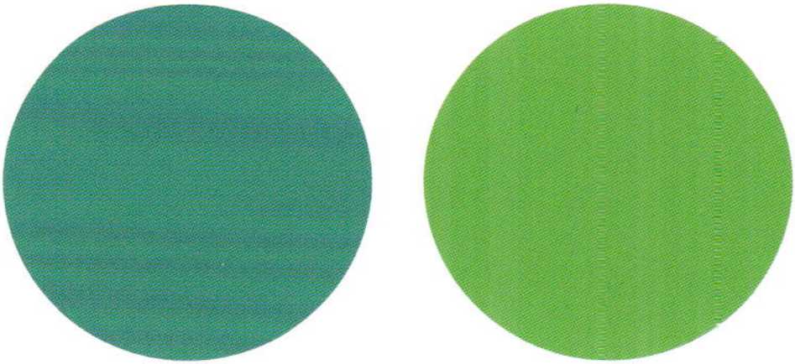

For example, both of these colors are green, but the green on the left contains an even 50% distribution of yellow and blue. The green on the right is 30% blue and 70% yellow. The higher amount of yellow makes the green on the right warmer than the one on the left.

A single color can be made up of both warm and cool tones. The only exception to this rule is orange, which is always considered a warm-toned color.

Warm vs. Cool Colors

Warm colors generally convey a sense of heat, passion, and energy. They tend to be more vibrant and command attention. The three primary warm colors are yellow, orange, and red.

Cool colors generally convey a sense of coldness, calm, and introspection. They tend to be more harmonious and peaceful. The three primary cool colors are green, blue, and violet.

Undertone

An **undertone** is when a color has a subtle, underlying hint of another color within it. While blue is a cool color, it can have a yellow undertone to it that makes it a little warmer than a pure blue. Adding just a tiny bit of red to a pure blue won't immediately turn it into purple, but it will give that blue a reddish undertone.

Neutral Colors

Neutral colors have roughly equal parts warm and cool tones, like some shades of ivory, beige, and brown. Black, white, and pure gray are not considered warm or cool, although you can add red, yellow, or blue to create a warm or cool undertoned gray.

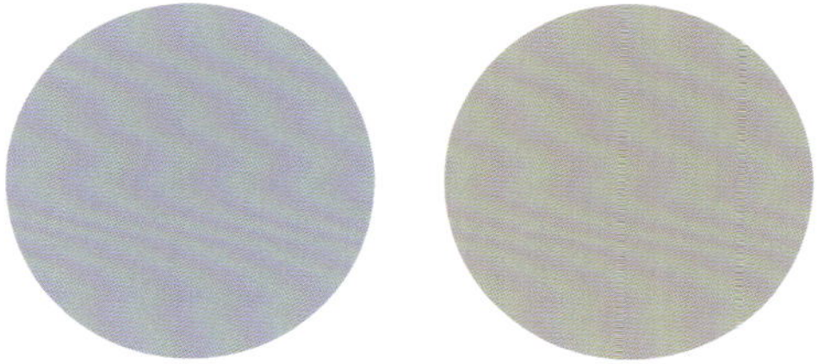

The gray on the left is cooler toned, while the gray on the right is warmer.

USING COLOR TEMPERATURE AND VALUE TO CREATE DEPTH

Warm colors advance toward the viewer, while cool colors tend to recede and look further away. By using warm colors in the foreground and cool colors in the background you can enhance the sense of depth in an image.

For example, adding a bit of blue tones to your backgrounds can give the viewer a sense of the background being further away.

You can also use darker, less saturated colors to convey a sense of depth. Lighter and brighter colors help make objects appear closer to a viewer.

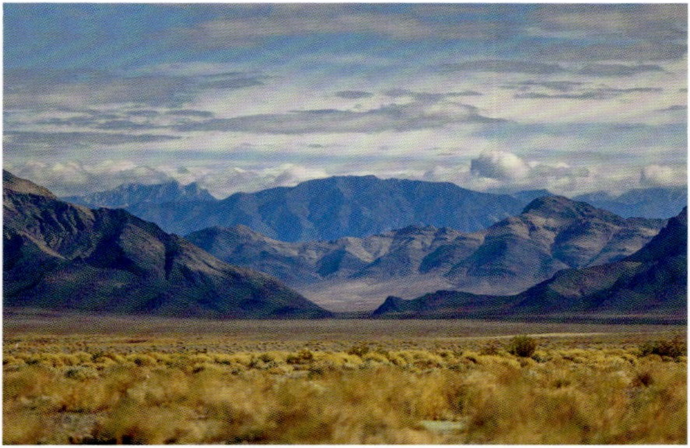

Notice how the mountains in this image become increasingly misty, less saturated, and cool toned the further away they are from the viewer. Comparatively, the elements in the foreground appear clearer, lighter, brighter, and warmer toned than elements in the background.

COLOR SCHEMES

A color scheme (also called a "color palette") is refers to a group of colors used within a work of art. When done correctly, color schemes help inform the viewer of the overall mood and theme of an art piece. The color wheel can help guide you in choosing a palette.

Analogous Colors

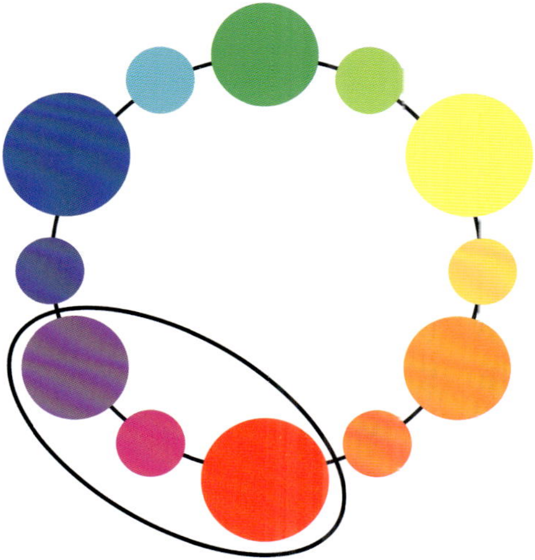

Analogous colors are next to one another on the color wheel. These color combinations tend to be more harmonious and lower contrast than complementary color palettes.

Complementary Colors

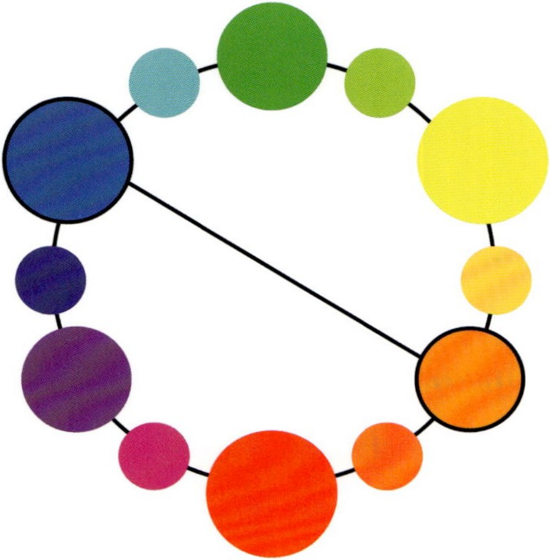

Complementary colors are directly opposite to one another on the color wheel. Complementary color combinations are high contrast, which means each color makes the other stand out when placed side by side. The result is a more vivid and eye-catching palette.

Split Complementary Colors

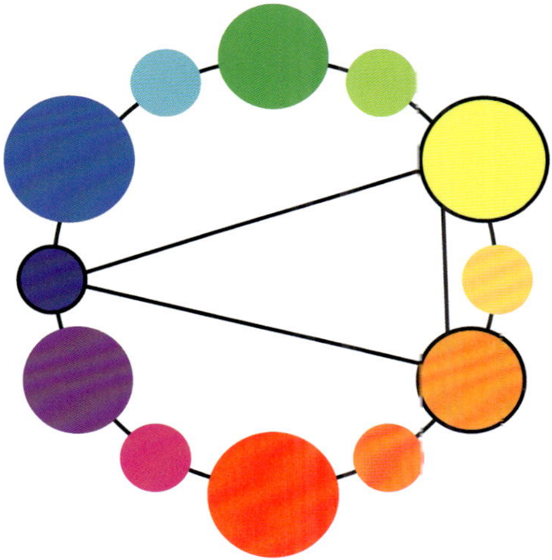

The **split complementary** color scheme involves choosing one color and then using the two colors adjacent to its complementary color on the color wheel.

Triad Colors

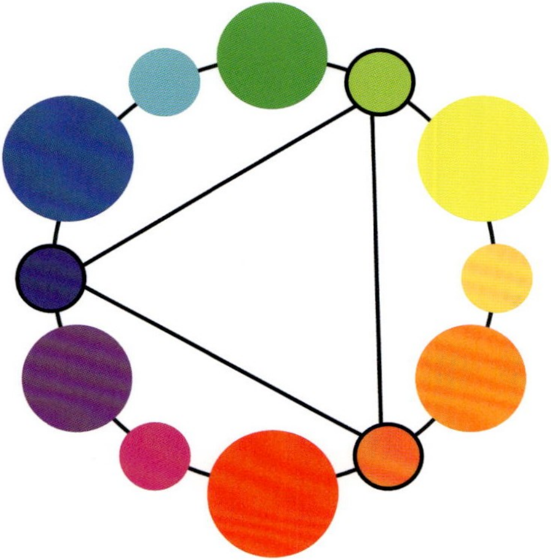

A **triadic** color scheme is formed by choosing three colors that are evenly spaced around the color wheel, forming a triangle. Two common triadic combinations are the primary colors (red, yellow, and blue) and the secondary colors (orange, green, and purple).

Square Colors

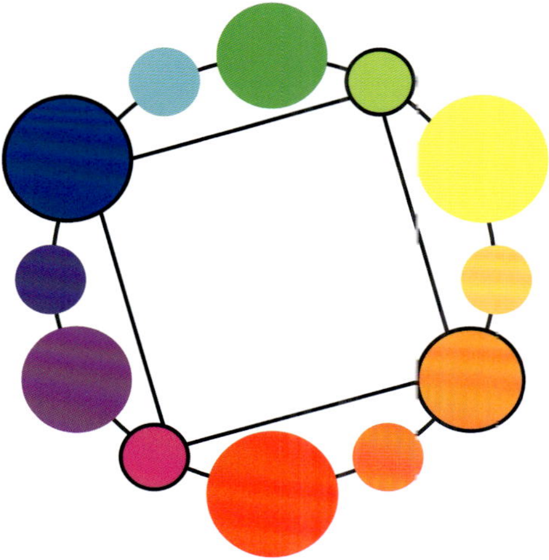

A **square** color scheme is formed by choosing four colors that are evenly spaced around the color wheel, forming a square.

Tetradic Colors

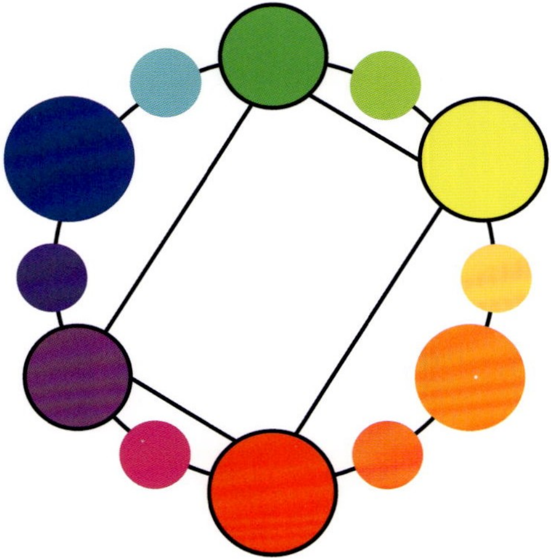

Similar to the square color scheme, the **tetradic** color scheme involves four colors, but in this scheme the colors form a rectangular shape on the color wheel.

Keep in mind that the more individual colors that are in your composition, the trickier it can be to manage. Square and tetradic color schemes have four colors and can pose a challenge for beginners, so it's a good idea to familiarize yourself with simpler color palettes first.

Monochromatic Colors

A **monochromatic** color scheme is made up of various shades, tints, and tones of the same base color. Monochromatic colors are great for beginners because they always result in a harmonious composition. An **achromatic** scheme is one without any colors at all, a scheme made up of white, black, and shades of gray.

05 BALANCING COLORS

Beyond how colors interact and balance each other, it's also important to think about how *much* of each color is present within a composition. Sometimes colors can compete with one another for a viewer's attention, or a color can get too muddy and blend into all the colors surrounding it. To ensure that an image has color harmony, some artists use proportions to keep the colors in their work balanced.

One way to do this is to organize your palette in a main color, one or more secondary colors, and an accent color. Oftentimes, the main color will be the least saturated and the most muted, while the accent color will be the most vivid. You can use your accent color to draw the viewer's eye to specific parts of your composition.

70/20/10

In a 70/20/10 scheme, the main color takes up 70% of the composition, the secondary color takes up 20%, and the accent color takes up 10%.

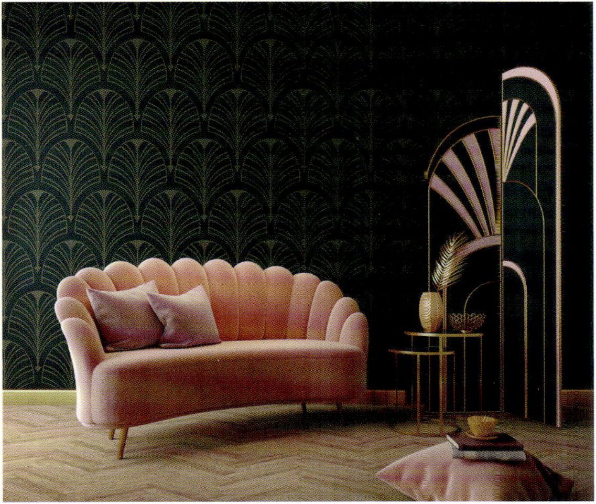

In this image, the main color is dark green and takes up most of the space. The two secondary colors are pink and beige, and the accent color is gold.

60/30/10

In a 60/30/10 scheme, the main color takes up 60% of the composition, the secondary color takes up 30%, and the accent color takes up 10%.

CMYK AND RGB

If you're producing artwork digitally or for print, it's important to understand the CMYK and RGB systems. Choosing correctly between CMYK and RGB will ensure your digitally produced art or printed artwork will look its best.

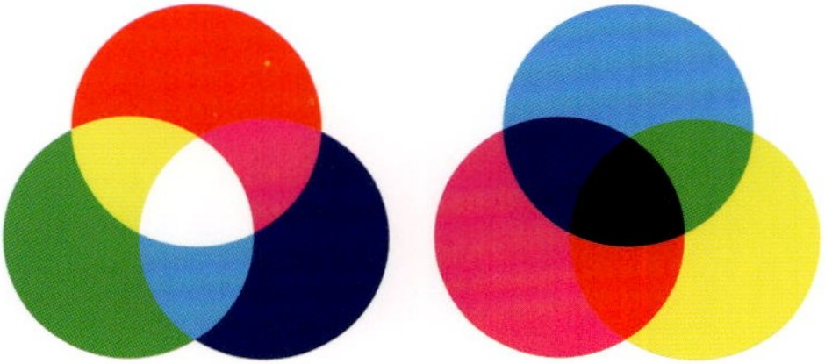

RGB CMYK

CMYK stands for **Cyan**, **Magenta**, **Yellow**, and **Black**. CMYK has over 16,000 color possibilities and is better for larger file formats. Because CMYK uses black for mixing, the colors tend to be somewhat less saturated. CMYK is the superior system for printing, and colors are more likely to come out as they appear on a screen when using CMYK. This is also due to the fact that white ink is not used in a CMYK system, since art is typically printed on white paper. Any areas that should be white in an artwork are printed with no ink whatsoever, so the white of the paper acts in place of white ink.

RGB stands for **Red**, **Green**, and **Blue**. Colors are brighter and more saturated in RGB compared to CMYK, because more than black can be used to blend colors together. For that reason RGB offers more than 16 million color possibilities. RGB is best for any media, art, or design that will be viewed on a digital device.

QUICK BEGINNER TIPS

- **Don't overdo it.** When you're new to the world of color theory, it can be easy to get overzealous and go a little overboard. It's common for newbies to introduce too many saturated or conflicting colors, or to go crazy with contrast. While colorful and high-contrast art can be wonderful, make sure you make these color choices intentionally and thoughtfully.

- **Take frequent breaks.** Human eyes tend to slowly get used to their surroundings over time. Even the most seasoned colorists sometimes make color choices that aren't ideal simply due to the fact that they've been staring too closely at their work for too long. Make sure that you're occasionally stopping and stepping back to look at your work from a distance. Doing this will allow you to catch and correct mistakes early. This is a good tip for making art in general, not just for using color.
- **Consider the lighting.** Sometimes it can be easy to default to a coloring method that has worked in the past without considering whether or not it's the best method for the composition you're working on. Let's say you're painting a landscape. It's important to remember that time of day will have a major impact on the lighting, and therefore, will have a major impact on the colors. The same field of flowers will look very different in the light at dusk, midday, and midnight, for example. Be sure to think about how the lighting in your composition influences your color choices.

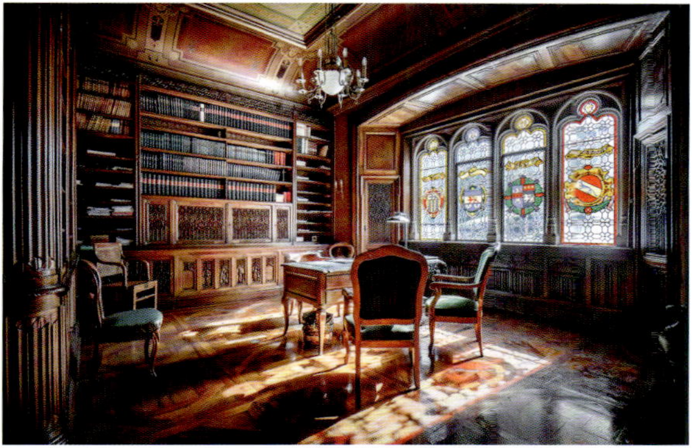

The dramatic lighting in this photo provides a lot of contrast and makes the space feel moodier and more mysterious.

- **Capture light with golden hour.** Also known as "magic hour," golden hour occurs right before sunset and right after sunrise. During this brief window of time, the lighting is warmer and significantly less harsh than midday sun lighting. The warmth and softness of golden hour is highly sought after amongst photographers and filmmakers.

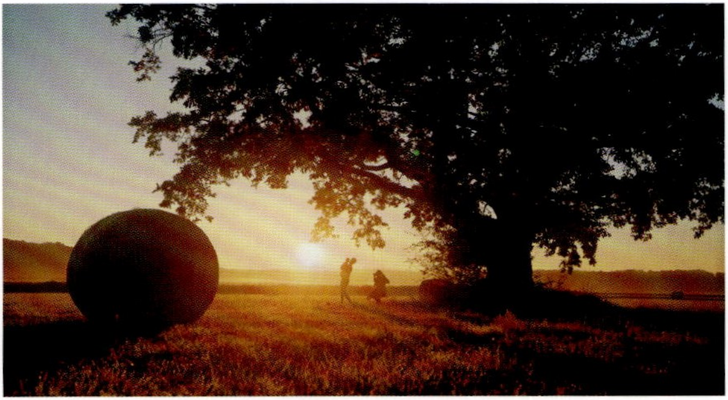

The low angle of the sun during golden hour suffuses a scene with warm glowing light.

- **Find cool colors in blue hour.** This occurs during the early twilight and dawn hours when the sun is below the horizon. The result is a soft or dimly lit and deeply saturated blue sky. This lighting is considered to be moody and mysterious. In the morning, blue hour gives way to golden hour, while in the evening it's the other way around.

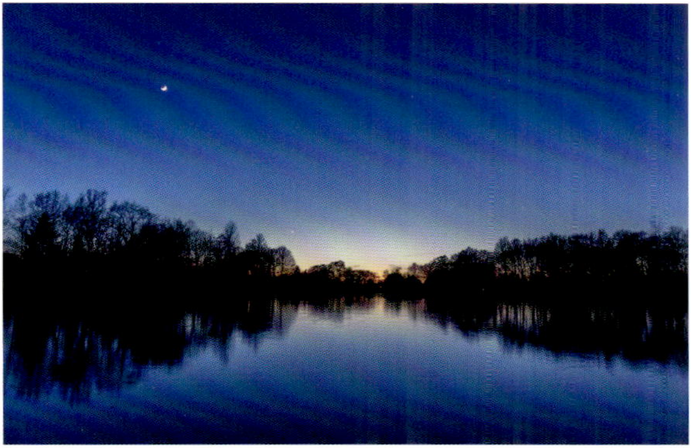

Blue hour adds a mysterious coolness to a scene. The sky becomes a deeply saturated blue with sunlight only hinted at on the horizon.

CONCLUSION

I hope this guide has helped you gain a basic understanding of color theory and how it can be harnessed to empower your work as an artist. Now, go out into the world and experiment! Create your own inspiring color palettes, and refer back to this guide whenever you need a refresher. Thanks for reading, and happy coloring!

ACKNOWLEDGEMENTS

A big thank you to my partner Ken, whose encouragement and support kept me going throughout the writing of this guide.

IMAGE CREDITS

Cover image: iStock.com/malerapaso

Page 5: iStock.com/Rixipix

Page 6: iStock.com/anyaivanova

Page 7: iStock.com/boggy22

Page 8: iStock.com/numismarty

Page 21: iStock.com/LPETTET

Page 30: iStock.com/Ninoon

Page 31: iStock.com/leonarth

Page 33: iStock.com/HannamariaH

Page 35: iStock.com/Gregory_DUBUS

Page 36: iStock.com/Sebastian Sonnen

Page 37: iStock.com/SimonSkafar